An Orange in January

Dianna Hutts Aston • illustrated by Julie Maren

Dial Books for Young Readers

In a land that glowed
with spring light,
an orange blossomed.

Bees feasted
on nectar sweet as honey,
until . . .

the petals fell away,
and the orange
began to grow
into what it was meant to be.

It grew slowly and steadily,
fed by the earth's soil
and the ocean's breath.

Soaked with rain
and drenched in sunshine,
the orange grew plump and bright,
until . . .

a hand, brown with seasons of sun,
plucked it from its branch,
while dew still glittered on the leaves.
Its days of growing were over . . .
but there was life in it yet,
and it still had far to go.

From bag
to basket,

truck
   to truck,

it followed the skyway
over mountains,
 across deserts and plains,
 until . . .

the orange arrived at a grocery store.
There it rested,
aglow with the goodness inside it,
  until . . .

two hands, small and soft,
took it from the pile,
and called it
the best one of all.

Carrying it home,
the child felt its roundness

and imagined himself

a juggler,

a pitcher,

a fortune-teller, who could see tomorrow.

That night,
as ice gleamed on the branches,
he dreamed
of a land that shone
in summer light.

When morning came,
the orange
reached the end of its journey,
bursting with the seasons inside it.

And two hands,
pink with cold,
shared its segments,

so that everyone
could taste
the sweetness of an orange in January.

DIAL BOOKS FOR YOUNG READERS • A division of Penguin Young Readers Group • Published by The Penguin Group
Penguin Group (USA) Inc., 375 Hudson Street, New York, NY 10014, U.S.A.
Penguin Group (Canada), 90 Eglinton Avenue East, Suite 700, Toronto, Ontario, Canada M4P 2Y3 (a division of Pearson Penguin Canada Inc.)
Penguin Books Ltd, 80 Strand, London WC2R 0RL, England
Penguin Ireland, 25 St. Stephen's Green, Dublin 2, Ireland (a division of Penguin Books Ltd)
Penguin Group (Australia), 250 Camberwell Road, Camberwell, Victoria 3124, Australia (a division of Pearson Australia Group Pty Ltd)
Penguin Books India Pvt Ltd, 11 Community Centre, Panchsheel Park, New Delhi - 110 017, India
Penguin Group (NZ), Cnr Airborne and Rosedale Roads, Albany, Auckland 1310, New Zealand (a division of Pearson New Zealand Ltd)
Penguin Books (South Africa) (Pty) Ltd, 24 Sturdee Avenue, Rosebank, Johannesburg 2196, South Africa
Penguin Books Ltd, Registered Offices: 80 Strand, London WC2R 0RL, England

Designed by Peonia Vázquez-D'Amico • Text set in Gill Sans
Manufactured in China on acid-free paper
2 4 6 8 10 9 7 5 3 1

Library of Congress Cataloging-in-Publication Data
Aston, Dianna Hutts.
An orange in January / Dianna Hutts Aston ; illustrated by Julie Maren.
p. cm.
Summary: An orange begins its life as a blossom where bees feast on the nectar,
and reaches the end of its journey, bursting with the seasons inside it, in the hands of a child.
ISBN-13: 978-0-8037-3146-2
[1. Oranges—Fiction.]   I. Maren, Julie, date, ill. II. Title.
PZ7.A8483Or 2007
[E]—dc22
2006014488

The illustrations were done in acrylic on bristol board.

To my friend
Christy Stallop,
with love
and gratitude.

—D.H.A.

For my precious
nephew, Shepherd.
Welcome to
the world!

—J.M.